# TRUMPET

# Best of
# Shrek and Shrek 2

## 12 Solo Arrangements with CD Accompaniment

**TRUMPET**

Arranged and Recorded by Bill Gulino

Cherry Lane Music Company
Director of Publications/Project Editor: Mark Phillips

ISBN 1-57560-799-9

*Visit our website at www.cherrylane.com*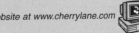

# CONTENTS

# ACCIDENTALLY IN LOVE

Words and Music by
Adam F. Duritz

TRUMPET

# ALL STAR

TRUMPET

Words and Music by
Greg Camp

# BEST YEARS OF OUR LIVES

TRUMPET

Words and Music by
David Jaymes and Geoffrey Deane

# FAIRY GODMOTHER SONG

Words and Music by
Andrew Adamson, Harry Gregson-Williams,
Stephen Barton, Dave Smith,
Walt Dohrn and Aron Warner

TRUMPET

# HOLDING OUT FOR A HERO

TRUMPET

Words by Dean Pitchford

Music by Jim Steinman

# I'M A BELIEVER

TRUMPET

Words and Music by
Neil Diamond

# I'M ON MY WAY

TRUMPET

Words and Music by
Charles Reid and Craig Reid

# IT IS YOU
## (I Have Loved)

TRUMPET

Words and Music by
Dana Glover, Harry Gregson-Williams,
John Powell and Gavin Greenaway

# LITTLE DROP OF POISON

TRUMPET

Words and Music by
Tom Waits and Kathleen Brennan

# LIVIN' LA VIDA LOCA

TRUMPET

Words and Music by
Robi Rosa and Desmond Child

# STAY HOME

TRUMPET

Words and Music by
Matt Mahaffey

**Moderately**

# YOU'RE SO TRUE

TRUMPET

Words and Music by
Joseph Arthur

15

# DreamWorks Pictures™

*Cherry Lane Music is proud to be the exclusive print music publisher for DreamWorks Pictures™. We are pleased to present folios and sheet music for the following critically acclaimed movies:*

### Almost Famous –Highlights

12 songs from the Grammy Award-winning soundtrack to the poignant movie that Cameron Crowe calls his "love letter back to music." This souvenir folio includes an introduction, photos from the film, hits from the '70s, and some songs from the repertoire of Stillwater, the fictional band portrayed in the movie. Songs include: America (Simon & Garfunkel) • Every Picture Tells a Story (Rod Stewart) • Fever Dog (Stillwater) • Lucky Trumble (Nancy Wilson) • Mr. Farmer (The Seeds) • That's the Way (Led Zeppelin) • Tiny Dancer (Elton John) • The Wind (Cat Stevens) • and more.

_____02500343  P/V/G..........................$14.95

### Amistad

*Score composed by John Williams*

Selections from the groundbreaking Steven Spielberg film include the resplendent main theme, "Dry Your Tears, Afrika." Also features photos from the film, as well as historical background and commentary from both Williams and Spielberg.

_____02501801  Piano/Vocal ................$14.95

### Gold and Glory: The Road to El Dorado

This beautiful souvenir songbook features full-color photos and 8 songs from the DreamWorks animated film. Includes original songs by Elton John and Tim Rice, and a score by Hans Zimmer and John Powell. Songs: Cheldorado – Score • El Dorado • Friends Never Say Goodbye • It's Tough to Be a God • Someday out of the Blue (Theme from El Dorado) • The Trail We Blaze • Without Question • Wonders of the New World: To Shibalba.

_____02500274  Easy Piano..................$14.95
_____02500273  P/V/G..........................$16.95

### Gladiator

*Music from the Motion Picture*

This terrific collection contains piano solo arrangements of 8 songs by Hans Zimmer and Lisa Gerrard from this summer's big blockbuster! Includes: Am I Not Merciful? • Barbarian Horde • The Battle • Earth • Honor Him • The Might of Rome • Now We Are Free • Slaves to Rome. Also includes a fantastic 8-page section featuring full-color photos from the film!

_____02500318  Piano Solo..................$12.95

### Prince of Egypt

*Original songs by Stephen Schwartz and Diane Warren*
*Score composed by Hans Zimmer*

Selections from the acclaimed DreamWorks animated film include all feature songs by Stephen Schwartz ("All I Ever Wanted," "Deliver Us," "When You Believe" and more) as well as themes from the Hans Zimmer soundtrack. Fully illustrated throughout with color reproductions of the stunning artwork!

_____02500026  P/V/G..........................$16.95
_____02500027  Easy Piano ................$14.95

*Also Available:*

_____02500028  Recorder Fun! ...........$9.95

*Prices, contents, and availability subject to change without notice.*

**CHERRY LANE MUSIC COMPANY**
6 East 32nd Street, New York, NY 10016
*Quality in Printed Music*

### Saving Private Ryan

*Score composed by John Williams*

Selections from the heralded Steven Spielberg film include the moving "Hymn to the Fallen." Plus color photos, historical and background information on the making of the film from Steven Spielberg, Tom Hanks, and other cast members.

_____02500072  Piano Solo ................$14.95

### Shrek

7 songs from the soundtrack of this innovative animated film. Includes: All Star • I'm a Believer • I'm on My Way • It Is You (I Have Loved) • Stay Home • True Love's First Kiss • You Belong to Me.

_____02500414  P/V/G..........................$14.95

## SHEET MUSIC

### For Always
(from *A.I.*)
_____02500449  Piano/Vocal ................$3.95

### Hymn to the Fallen
(from *Saving Private Ryan*)
_____02500030  Piano/Vocal ................$3.95

### Someday Out of the Blue
(Elton John)
(Theme from *The Road to El Dorado*)
_____02500289  Piano/Vocal ................$3.95

### When You Believe
(Whitney Houston & Mariah Carey)
(from *Prince of Egypt*)
_____02500082  P/V/G ..........................$3.95
_____02500109  Easy Piano ................$3.95

EXCLUSIVELY DISTRIBUTED BY

HAL•LEONARD® CORPORATION
7777 W. BLUEMOUND RD. P.O. BOX 13819 MILWAUKEE, WI 53213

Visit Cherry Lane on the Internet at **www.cherrylane.com**